Look How Tall I Am!

Tessa Patel

Illustrated by Teresa Culkin-Lawrence

We have a growth chart
at our house. We use it
to measure how tall we are.

2

3

Dad measures me.

"Look how tall I am!" I say.

"Now it's Ben's turn," says Dad.

Dad measures Ben.

"Look how tall I am!" says Ben.

"Now it's Ryan's turn," I say.
Dad measures Ryan.

"Look how tall I am!" says Ryan.

"Carmen is the tallest," says Ben. "Ryan and I are both shorter than Carmen!"

4 —Carmen 7
—Carmen 6
—Ben 5
— Carmen 5

—Carmen 4
3 — Ben 3
— Ryan 3
— Carmen 2

— Ben 2

2 Ben 1
— Carmen 1
— Ryan 1

1

11

"We will see about that," laughs Dad.
He puts Ryan on Ben's shoulders.

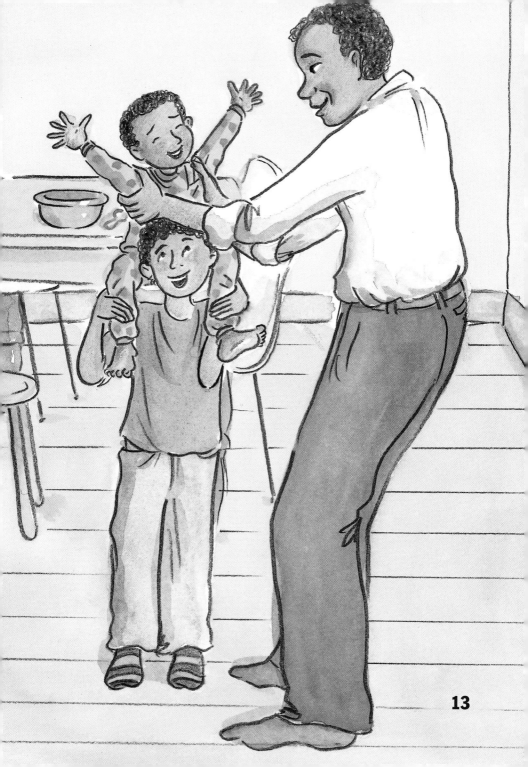

I stand next to Ben and Ryan.
I laugh, "Now I'm the shortest!"

15

"But Dad is the tallest of all!"
we say.